GILES LAROCHE

WHAT'S INSIDE?

Fascinating Structures Around the World

HOUGHTON MIFFLIN BOOKS FOR CHILDREN

Houghton Mifflin Harcourt

Boston 2009

At the end of a long underground passageway an archaeologist opens this sealed door. Leading to a series of hidden chambers, the door has not been opened in nearly three thousand years.

WHAT'S INSIDE?

NAME:
Tomb of Tutankamun

LOCATION:
Valley of the Kings,
Nile River,
Thebes, Egypt

**DATE OF
CONSTRUCTION:**
1327 BC

DEPTH:
Four rooms 8 to 10
feet (2.5–3 meters)
high, buried 25 feet
(7.6 meters) under-
ground

MATERIALS:
Hewn out of a
limestone hillside

TODAY:
Treasures from the
tomb can be seen
at the Egyptian
Museum in Cairo.

**LITTLE KNOWN
FACT:**
Sealed boxes
found in the tomb
contained raisins,
dates, nuts,
watermelon seeds,
cakes, bread,
cereals, onions,
and meat.

In 1922, the archaeologist Howard Carter discovered King Tutankamun's tomb, placed in underground vaults to survive the ages, its sole entry hidden and sealed from robbers. The treasures included the king's mummy, a painted wood statue of his head, gold and silver chests and chariots, chairs, even food. The ancient Egyptians believed in a life after death and provided their deceased with all of the necessities and sometimes luxuries for their afterlife. Tutankhamun became the Pharaoh, or king of Egypt, at the age of nine, and he ruled for nearly ten years.

King Tut's tomb is hidden underground, but this brightly painted building was constructed on the rocky crest of a hill so it could always be seen silhouetted against the sky. Monumental rows of Doric columns support triangular pediments at each end and surround a sanctuary that shelters a statue of this Greek city's namesake.

WHAT'S INSIDE?

NAME:

The Parthenon, or Temple of Athena Polias

LOCATION:

On the Acropolis, Athens, Greece

DATE OF CONSTRUCTION:

447–438 BC; badly damaged in a 1687 explosion

HEIGHT:

60 feet (18.3 meters) high, and 500 feet (152.5 meters) above the Aegean Sea. The forty-six marble columns are 34.5 feet (10.5 meters) high. The statue of Athena is 40 feet (12.2 meters) high.

MATERIALS:

Pentellic marble with iron clamps, wood and terra cotta for the roof.

ARCHITECTS:

Iktinos and Callicrates, under the leadership of the ruler Pericles

SCULPTOR:

Pheidias

TODAY:

Temple restoration continues. New marble stones in place are a slightly different color so the ancient can be distinguished from the modern. The statue of Athena has been missing since Roman times, but a small version is on display in the National Museum of Athens.

LITTLE KNOWN FACT:

The Parthenon was originally painted in shades of blue, ocher, and gold.

An ivory and gold statue of the goddess Athena stands tall inside the temple built to honor her. According to Greek mythology, Athena presented this important Greek city with an olive tree that she had created to provide food and lamplight from olive oil. Because the gift was so appreciated by the citizens, they gave their city, Athens, her name and made her its protector.

This structure, a square-based, stepped pyramid, is also dramatically silhouetted against the sky. It rises like a man-made mountain above a flat jungle. In this jungle roamed fierce cats held in awe by the builders of the pyramid. A small door at the bottom opens to a steep stairway barely big enough to walk through. This pitch-dark passage ascends to a secret chamber where a pair of gleaming eyes reflects the light of carried torches.

WHAT'S INSIDE?

NAME:
Temple of Kukulcan, or El Castillo

LOCATION:
Chichen Itza, northern Yucatan Peninsula, Mexico

DATE OF CONSTRUCTION:
850 AD

HEIGHT:
75 feet (22.8 meters) The jaguar throne is approximately 2 feet (.61 meters) high.

MATERIALS:
Quarried stone from limestone bedrock

TODAY:
The temple and stone jaguar can be visited, among many other buildings at Chichen Itza.

LITTLE KNOWN FACT:
The four stairways each have 91 steps, plus one at the top for a total of 365 steps — one for each day of the year.

A red throne in the shape of a jaguar sits in a chamber inside this Mayan temple. The jaguar's spots and yellow eyes are made of a rare local stone called jade. Archaeologists believe this massive temple was built to thank the gods for protecting the Mayan people from storms, earthquakes, comets, and other natural disasters. This throne was provided for the use of Kukulcan, God of the Wind, one of the earth's creators.

Halfway around the world from the Mayan temple is another kind of temple, a towering octagonal structure called a pagoda. Wind bells hang from the widely projecting eaves at each of the five main levels, and sculptures of lions guard the entrance. This pagoda and the statues inside were built to honor a beloved teacher who was the founder of one of the world's great religions.

WHAT'S INSIDE?

NAME:

Sakyamuni Pagoda or the Wooden Pagoda

LOCATION:

Fogong (Buddha's Palace) Temple, Yingxian County of Shanxi Province, China

DATE OF CONSTRUCTION:

1056 AD

MATERIALS:

Built entirely of wood on a brick base and painted ocher and blue with red pillars

HEIGHT:

220 feet (67.1 meters) tall, divided into five stories on the exterior with nine interior levels; the statue is 35 feet (10.6 meters) high.

TODAY:

After more than 950 years of exposure to rain, sun, lightning, and earthquakes, the pagoda has an uncertain future. Efforts are under way to restore it and prevent further damage. It is a UNESCO World Heritage Site.

LITTLE KNOWN FACT:

No nails were used in the pagoda's constuction.

A large statue of the renowned teacher and philosopher Siddhartha Gautama Buddha (c. 563–483 BC) sits on the ground floor of this house of worship. Each of the four levels above has three more seated Buddhas, enclosed by walls covered with murals, relics, and scriptures. Pagodas were often built as symbols of protection from natural disasters. This pagoda, one of the tallest and oldest wooden structures in the world, has withstood many earthquakes in its nearly one-thousand-year history.

This entry gate has an arched opening in the shape of a horseshoe.
A passageway for people and animals, it opens onto a large area surrounded by massive fortified walls built to protect the inhabitants and
their grand buildings and treasures from invasions.

WHAT'S INSIDE?

A whole city! Beyond the arch in the Puerta del Sol (Gate of the Sun) lies the walled Spanish city of Toledo, founded by the Romans, colonized by the Moors, and then conquered by the Christians. The Moors developed many unusual architectural forms, including the horseshoe

arch, shown in the entry gate. Here we see the painter El Greco
(1541–1614), who lived and worked in Toledo most of his life, carrying
his sketches through the maze of narrow streets lined with tiled-roofed
houses, palaces, and churches.

Shaped like the bow of a Spanish galleon and also surrounded by massive walls, this building and its watchtowers are perched high above the point where two rivers meet to form a natural moat. Containing a throne, works of art, and elaborate decoration and furnishings demanded

by a royal family, this castle is home to a powerful ruler forever linked to the European exploration of America.

WHO'S INSIDE?

NAME:
Alcazar (castle) of Segovia

LOCATION:
Segovia, Castilla La Mancha, Spain

DATE OF CONSTRUCTION:
Thirteenth to fifteenth century, restored in nineteenth century

MATERIALS:
Primarily stone and slate

BUILDERS:
King Alfonso X, King John II, and King Philip II

TODAY:
On a hill 262 feet (79.9 meters) above the castle moat, visitors may climb the 152 steps to the top of the alcazar's keep (square tower at left).

LITTLE KNOWN FACT:
The castle at Disneyland was modeled after the Alcazar of Segovia.

Isabella, wife of King Ferdinand of Spain, is preparing for the procession from her castle to a nearby church for the coronation ceremony crowning her queen of Castile. Years later she famously pledged her jewels to cover the cost of Christopher Columbus's first voyage across the Atlantic. On this voyage in 1492 Columbus encountered land and the native peoples of the Americas, although he believed he was in eastern Asia.

Free of defensive walls and built on a busy city street, this tower — with a clock, belfry, and spire — rises high above the building it tops to overlook a new city. In the belfry hangs the Liberty Bell, and in a room below an important meeting took place in 1776.

WHO'S INSIDE?

NAME:
Independence Hall

LOCATION:
Philadelphia, Pennsylvania

DATE OF CONSTRUCTION:
1732–56; current spire added in 1828

MATERIALS:
Primarily brick and wood

HEIGHT:
168 feet (51.2 meters)

ARCHITECTS:
Edmund Woolley, Andrew Hamilton, William Strickland (spire)

TODAY:
Independence Hall and the Liberty Bell are part of Independence National Historic Park.

LITTLE KNOWN FACT:
The already cracked Liberty Bell, hung in 1753, was removed in 1846 when the crack worsened. It is now on display at the Liberty Bell Center.

Here we see Ben Franklin (standing center) and the future presidents Thomas Jefferson (seated far right) and John Adams (standing far left) discussing America's Declaration of Independence with other members of the declaration committee. Originally built to serve as the statehouse for the colonial government of Pennsylvania, Independence Hall is now acclaimed as the birthplace of the United States of America.

In place of a lofty spire, this large round building in a small New England village has a squat wooden cupola at the top and is home to many forms of life.

WHAT'S INSIDE?

NAME:
Shaker dairy barn

LOCATION:
Hancock, Massachusetts

DATE OF CONSTRUCTION:
1826–70

MATERIALS:
Stone, brick, wood, glass. The walls are 21 feet (6.4 meters) high and 3.5 feet (1.1 meters) thick. The barn is 270 feet (82.3 meters) around.

TODAY:
The barn is open to visitors at Hancock Shaker Village.

LITTLE KNOWN FACT:
The Shakers also designed their own farm tools, furniture, and many other items of everyday use. Their famous designs are still produced today.

Horses, cattle, geese, chickens, and other farm animals make this circular barn their home. The animals live in connecting wings on the lower level of the barn surrounding a center space filled with hay. Threshers and wagons are stored on the upper level. The barn is round to avoid the wasted space of corners. Its builders, a religious group called the Shakers, were more concerned with the efficient use of materials than unnecessary or fancy decoration.

This canvas structure is also round and it too contains and covers diverse forms of life. It has a pointed top and festive banners. Every few days, it is dismantled, taken to a new location, and reassembled. People holding tickets are waiting to get in.

WHAT'S INSIDE?

NAME:
Circus tent
or "big top"

LOCATION:
Circuses traveled to many American cities, usually by train, and had winter homes in Florida.

DATE OF CONSTRUCTION:
Early-eighteenth to mid-nineteenth century.

MATERIALS:
Canvas, wood or metal poles, and rope, with a sawdust or dirt floor

ARCHITECT:
Joshua Purdy Brown introduced the circus tent in 1825, enabling the circus to travel from city to city with its own structure.

TODAY:
The show goes on.

LITTLE KNOWN FACT:
The use of canvas tents greatly diminished in the 1950s, when circuses began using arenas.

. A circus! And when the ringmaster cracks his whip in the air, the music begins, people fly like birds, elephants wearing spangled blankets perform tricks, tigers jump through golden rings, horses dance, and jugglers balance their act on a tightrope. Made of canvas, with poles to support the top, circus tents could easily be taken down and set up again at the next site. They were round so the surrounding crowd could see all the action.

Wedged between the typical rectangular buildings of a big city block, this building is round too! People come here to look at famous and valuable objects hanging on the walls, illuminated by a domed skylight.

WHAT'S INSIDE?

NAME:
Solomon R. Guggenheim Museum

LOCATION:
Fifth Avenue, New York City

DATE OF CONSTRUCTION:
1959

MATERIALS:
Primarily steel and concrete — with glass for the dome

ARCHITECT:
Frank Lloyd Wright

TODAY:
The museum is visited for both its architecture and its art.

LITTLE KNOWN FACT:
The architect intended visitors to ride elevators to the top of the museum and view the art while descending the spiraling ramps.

Hundreds of paintings! Spiraling ramps allow people to gradually ascend or descend the Guggenheim Museum while viewing the artwork on the walls. Because the building is round, paintings can be seen from many different viewpoints. Here, schoolchildren are looking at the paintings of Picasso, Kandinsky, and Klee in a museum with ever-changing exhibitions of modern and contemporary artists.

When the Guggenheim Museum opened on its big city block, construction of this dramatic building began on the opposite side of the world, on a point overlooking a city's harbor. When seen against the blue waters it makes people think of billowing sails or giant seashells. People come here mainly to listen.

WHAT'S INSIDE?

NAME:

Sydney Opera House

LOCATION:

Bennelong Point,
Sydney, Australia

**DATE OF
CONSTRUCTION:**

1959–73

MATERIALS:

Pre-stressed
concrete and glass,
with ceramic tiles
covering the shells.
The total area of
glass is 1.5 acres
(.06 hectares).

ARCHITECT:

Jorn Utzon

TODAY:

The opera house
is Sydney's most
distinctive landmark
and home to music,
opera, and theater.

**LITTLE KNOWN
FACT:**

Because of the
complex design, it
took twelve years
to build the
opera house.

Music! Here, Queen Elizabeth of Great Britain, seated in the royal box, attends the gala opening of the Sydney Opera House to hear a performance of Beethoven's Ninth Symphony. The architect designed the

sculptural shell shapes to house the various concert halls and theaters of this vast complex. It has since become a famous visual symbol of the Australian city.

These dual skyscrapers are also a symbol of their city. Looking like an enormous temple or giant identical pagodas, they are filled with activity — like a vertical city with elevators always going up and down.

WHAT'S INSIDE?

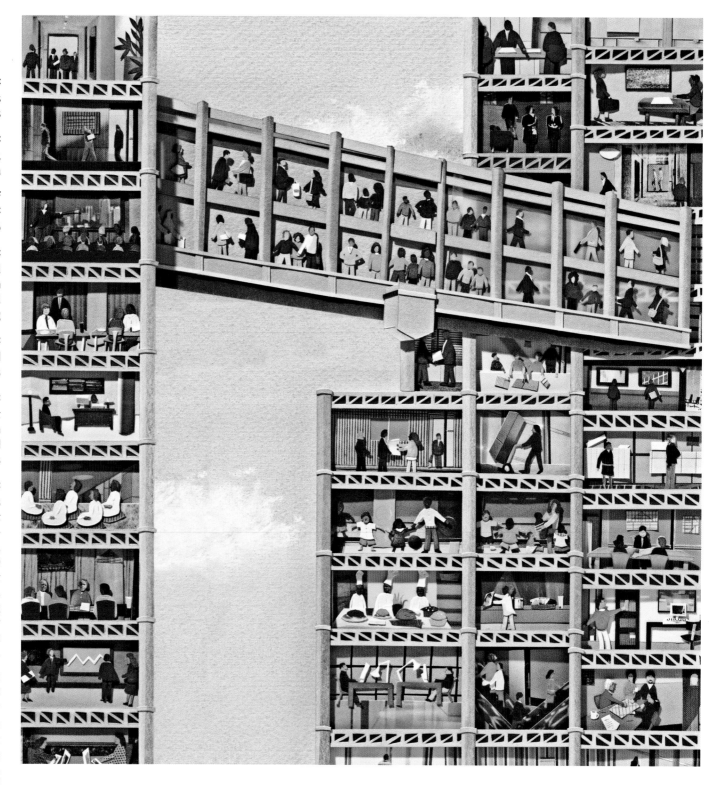

NAME:
Petronas
Twin Towers

LOCATION:
Kuala Lumpur,
Malaysia

**DATE OF
CONSTRUCTION:**
1996

MATERIALS:
Primarily steel
and glass, with
stainless-steel
cladding

ARCHITECT:
Cesar Pelli and
Associates

HEIGHT:
1,483 feet
(452 meters), with
88 floors and
32,000 windows

TODAY:
Visitors can cross
the Sky Bridge that
connects the sky-
scrapers. Together,
they contain 270
shops, an 840-seat
concert hall, cinemas,
and a revolving
restaurant. Over
20,000 people work
in Petronas Towers.

**LITTLE KNOWN
FACT:**
Petronas Towers'
plan is based on an
Islamic geometric
pattern symbolizing
unity, harmony,
stability, and
rationality.

Thousands of people! Floor after floor of people work in the hundreds of offices, watch movies in theaters, hear concerts, dine in the revolving restaurant at the top, and ride the many elevators. Petronas Towers, among the tallest buildings in the world, are joined by a bridge connecting the forty-first and forty-second floors, making them one building. This skyscraper in Malaysia dwarfs the monorail below that brings people to the tower from miles away.

Designed in the shape of a ship breaking a wave, this unusual building was constructed in a landlocked city — but its interior is largely filled with water.

What's Inside?

NAME:
Georgia Aquarium

LOCATION:
Atlanta, Georgia

DATE OF CONSTRUCTION:
2004–5.
It was built in 27 months.

MATERIALS:
Primarily steel, glass, and concrete

ARCHITECT:
Ventulett, Stainback, and Associates

TODAY:
Visitors can walk along a 100-foot-long glass tunnel through the aquarium — almost like walking under the sea.

LITTLE KNOWN FACT:
The main aquarium glass weighs 328 tons (297,824 kilograms) and holds 8 million gallons (30.2 million liters) of water.

More than a hundred thousand sea creatures swim, crawl, and float in millions of gallons of water in the Georgia Aquarium in Atlanta. The life forms displayed in gigantic tanks include hungry whale sharks, graceful beluga whales, sea lions, giant octopi, squid, viper fish, angelfish,

blowfish, turtles, shrimp, and countless tiny snails. Here we see two whale sharks in the ocean voyager display swimming along with two kinds of rays, hammerhead sharks, saw fish, a school of golden trevally, and several turquoise wrasse.

On this town street you can spot architectural details featured in the buildings in this book. Look for arches, columns, pediments, stairways, eaves, a gate, a cupola — even a tower with a light on.

Can you guess what might be inside the lit room?

GLOSSARY OF ARCHITECTURAL TERMS

ACROPOLIS

In Greek, "high city." The prominent point where the most important temples and public buildings stand.

ALCAZAR

A Spanish word for a fortified house or palace, from the Arabic word *al-qasr*.

ARCH

A curved support over an opening to transfer a weight above. The arch, developed by the Romans, was unknown to both the ancient Greeks and Mayans. A later example is the horseshoe arch, which widens after its curve begins and narrows to a round or pointed top.

BELFRY

A section of a tower where a bell is hung, as in Independence Hall. From *berfrei*, an old French word for *tower*.

CHAMBER

An enclosed space, sometimes hidden, as the chambers of King Tut's tomb.

COLUMN

A supporting shaft to a weight above. The Doric columns of the Parthenon are built in ten to twelve sections called drums and are anchored by iron clamps. *Doric* refers to a region of Greece where these types of columns (fluted with no base) originated.

CUPOLA

A very small dome that is round, square, or even octagonal in shape. It is placed above a larger dome, spire, or barn, and is often topped with a weathervane. A cupola may have windows or vents to allow light to enter or to let air circulate.

DOME

A curved structure forming a canopy over a space, which sits on a base. A dome is sometimes made of glass, allowing natural light to fill the space below.

EAVE

The underpart of a roof's edge projecting over a wall to shed rain and create shade. A pagoda's curved eaves often project much farther than those of other structures, requiring the support of a column and bracket called a dougong, which is often elaborately carved and painted.

FORTRESS

A strong, secure place or structure built for defense.

GALLEON

A Spanish square-rigged sailing ship of the fifteenth century, used for trade and exploration. A galleon had the appearance of a floating castle.

GATE

An opening in a wall, fence, or other enclosure, allowing entry or exit. It may be simple, elaborate, or celebratory, symbolizing the place it serves.

KEEP

The most secure part of a medieval castle, often a large tower. The keep served as the main living quarters of a castle during a siege. Also called a dungeon, it could be used as a prison.

LIMESTONE

A sedimentary rock used throughout history as a building material. Limestone is formed by the accumulation of seashells, coral, fossils, sand, and silt that form the mineral calcite. Its color varies from almost white to gray and ocher.